Mexica Mix
Marina Sánchez

VERVE
POETRY PRESS
BIRMINGHAM

PUBLISHED BY VERVE POETRY PRESS
https://vervepoetrypress.com
mail@vervepoetrypress.com

All rights reserved
© 2021 Marina Sánchez

The right of Marina Sánchez to be identified as author of this work has been asserted in accordance with section 77 of the Copyright, Designs and Patents Act 1988.

No part of this work may be reproduced, stored or transmitted in any form or by any means, graphic, electronic, recorded or mechanical, without the prior written permission of the publisher.

FIRST PUBLISHED MAR 2021

Printed and bound in the UK
by Positive Print, Birmingham

ISBN: 978-1-912565-52-8

'To my parents and ancestors for the gift of life; to the Earth for being home; to all my teachers, especially Gloria Anzaldúa and to all those who are part of the healing of the world.'

CONTENTS

I) Family

For my Father Each Time He Crossed Pyrenees	6
Colonial History	8
Clouds of Doubt	9
Where Are you Going?	10
Watching Mother's Ninety-Year-Old Heart	11
Considerations when Curating the Past	13
Bodies of Water	14
Born in the year of the Dragon	15
Milk	16
They Said Many Things	17
My Daughter's Knight	18

II) Icons

Black Madonna	19
¡Ay Dios Mío!	20
Malintzin Tenépal, Malinalli: Revised	22
In the Name of la Santa Muerte	24
Duel between Quetzalcoatl and Tezcatlipoca	26
Iztli Tezcatl*	27

III) Earth

Riviera Maya	29
The Axolotls	30
Exiled Monarch	31
Tlililtzin/ Campanitas	32
Wall	33
Dark Earth	34
Arctic Circle	36
Blessing: Spring 2020	37

Acknowledgements

Mexica Mix

I) Family

For my Father Each Time he Crossed the Pyrenees

Many years gone, I wish he'd worn
wool socks, home-spun with burrs
still attached, knitted by someone
who hoped he'd wear them out.

I wish he'd worn leather boots,
a proper pair, thick hide, well-stitched.
Though they might have become hardened,
with that white deposit caked all over,

his feet would have been dry as he trudged
through snow and mud, up to peaks,
down to passes, his breath quick,
heart pounding, that tightness in his chest.

I wish he'd worn a good leather jacket,
stiff, heavy, three-quarter length,
for keeping out the winter of '39.
Was he wearing the Basque *boina* he kept?

For the week's trek, I wish he'd carried
home-cooked food in his satchel:
tortilla, bread, chorizo and jamón,
a slice of membrillo, tinto in a bottle.

Though he's been gone many years,
I still wish he'd had to cross only once,
to avoid the grief of the *emigrante*.
Instead the load grew heavier,

until his heart could bear no more.
Latour-de-Carol, Bourg Madame,
Prats-de-Mollo-La-Preste,
Le Perthus, Cerbère.

Colonial History

The names of the dishes still sing in my mouth:
                         Chiles en Nogada   Tamales   Chalupas
Just as dad was exiled from Spain, Mexican food
                         was exiled from our table:
Quesadillas   Mole Poblano   Chilaquiles

I grew up wondering about the Chiles*
            in the creamy sauce, scattered with pomegranate seeds,
heard stories of how *abuelita** would spend days
                   preparing the *Mole* and pounding
twenty-four types of chillies and dark chocolate.

                   I grew up with mum & dad's explosions
when we drove past the Spanish churches
                 built on top of the pyramids in Cholula.
These eruptions were followed by his silences,
             her slamming doors and me tiptoeing around

these volcanoes. But mealtimes were another
               arena for their quarrels: her branding dad
el conquistador, him cursing her Indian pride
              retaliating that if his ancestors hadn't arrived,
Mexicans would still be wearing loincloths.
             So, while these fierce warriors dished out colonial
history, I imagined what we were missing.

---

*Chiles: green peppers   ** Abuelita:* granny

Clouds of Doubt

Mother's mouth was a story-telling flower,
painted in her favourite bougainvillea
lipstick, conjuring clouds of doubt
about where she was born.

Sometimes she'd say it was Cuernavaca,
'the city of eternal spring',
on the slopes of her beloved volcanoes
and the Chichinatzin mountains,

where dad would stop to buy her orchids.
Other times, she'd say we came from Mixtecs.
But she looked down on *'indios'* and *'prietos'*,
only pointing out her skin colour

to boast how she turned *chocolate* in the sun.
While she resented my questions,
what else could I do? As a child,
I felt the weight she carried,

how she seemed trapped in her game
of concealing and revealing,
then sighs, quick laughter, silence.
My ancestors lie like budbursts in these tales.

Indios: native Indians from one of the many indigenous tribes in Mexico - *Prietos*: slang for someone who has dark skin

Where are you going?

After father died, mother spoke a new tongue:
hers was the grammar of tears, sighs and cries,
the syntax of silence, one long sentence of grief.
She thrust towards me her dictionary of fears.

She raged at home, in the market and in the street,
she railed against God (though never in church):
¿Porqué se lo llevó Dios?
She cursed her luck: *¡Mi puta y rechingada suerte!*

But she stopped when the glinting of tracks
in the underground hypnotised her,
sometimes taking a step forward towards them.
Then I'd hold her hand tighter: *¿Adónde vas?*

Watching Mother's Ninety-Year-Old Heart

Her heart beats monochrome at first,
within the open fan shape of the scan.

The technician taps blue and red
for blood, then yellow, orange, purple.

I want to ask what they mean
but I'm hushed by his silence.

The grainy images spread and spike
with a tired thrumming in my ears.

I stare at one of the four mouths, closing,
opening, the dark rush flowing in and out.

Each wet, sucking pulse seems such an effort.
Then back to him measuring the valves.

This one is slightly slower than the others,
misses its turn to open and close.

That's where the blood might have pooled,
congealed, become stagnant,

a missile circulating in her body,
damaging the brain when it settled.

But they're still not sure.
When his face is no longer lit

by views of my mother's heart,
he leaves, whispering to himself.

As she sleeps in this dark threshold,
I run my hand through the silver field of her hair,

her heartbeat like the metronome
when she played the piano.

Considerations When Curating the Past

Sorting and divvying family photos,
my sister and I find an old envelope.
There's a picture of mother and father
before they were married,
he's smiling, his arm around her.

Her face makes us shudder.
It's the only photo we've discovered
where she looks as we remember her.
Rose pushes it away,
but I add it to my pile.

Oh, I really want to tear it up.
But if I do, what of the past?
Her rain of stinging slaps on face and body,
lashing us with dad's belt after he died,
those caustic remarks that choked us.

Though some say that what endures needs
no pictures, I am left holding this proof
that belongs with all the unhinged,
wild and unmoored parts of the story
that are not known, spoken or heard.

Bodies of Water

What if language was a body of water
flowing through us from birth, where we drink,
swim and sail? Or what if through our lives
we needed to learn the ways of another
lake, river or stream, its depth and currents,

its temperament through the seasons,
how to read the light and sky
as they shade and shadow water,
how it takes time to feel safe as creatures
that adapt where others belong,

whether hugged by mountains,
springing up as an oasis
or aching for the mouth of the river.
What if language was a body of water
where we only stay in the shallows,

though we yearn to become more fluent
in our sleek and slender words,
abandoning ourselves, like otters,
to our mother current.
But wherever we paddle or swim,

we hear, taste and feel from source to mouth,
that urgent call, so we brave rapids,
plunge down waterfalls and surge
from deep aquifers in barren lands,
unafraid of silence, unafraid of drowning.

Born in the Year of the Dragon

For years it had hung near her father's heart:
a lozenge of Han imperial jade, where
a coiled dragon raised its head above
the dark green stone, crowning the carving.
A creature mediating between the worlds.

The moon was full, sharks and surfers stayed away.
But no, his auspicious amulet would never
be ripped by the muscular waves. Bleeding,
we tumbled out, stung by the slap of salt.
We looked for it as the tide sucked pebbles

back as quickly as we turned them over,
like when she was born, we searched
for reasons, unreasons, threads of causality,
for the differences she kept revealing,
sought answers from what we gleaned

doctors couldn't or wouldn't say.
Later we learnt they didn't know.
In those early days someone remarked,
as people do when almost all seems lost,
that *'of course she'll be fine, besides*

she was born in the year of the dragon,
the luckiest of all'. But instead of accepting
a chaotic universe, I go back to the roar
of that Pacific beach, to make sense of luck,
of what nature grabbed one year, gave back the next.

Milk

For the rocks that were my breasts,
the midwife suggested cold cabbage leaves,
someone else Mackeson, another Guinness.
I thought the skin would burst when veins
surfaced like rivers seen from a satellite.

While my daughter lay in Intensive Care,
a few hours old, a nurse shoved
a plastic hand pump in my chest, pointed
to a cupboard. I managed a thimbleful.
Pobrecita, she couldn't latch on, couldn't suck.

I learnt to tube feed her every three hours.
Then I was allowed to take her home.
She became heavier to hold,
her eyes less sunken,
her cheeks rounded when she smiled.

Some even called her plump, which sustained me
when getting up at night, the only sound
was the whooshing of the pump's pistons.
I thought of other mothers in the dark.
Afterwards, the silence was a loud emptiness.

Blood becoming milk reminded me
how far I was from those old paintings
I'd seen as a child of Madonnas and myths,
the goddess nursing her infant, squeezing
the Milky Way out of her breast.

They said many things

After she was born and they took her blood
on the hour, I'd hold her closer,
even though the nurses warned:
'When she grows up,
she'll always think of you with pain'.

Whenever she had surgery, they said:
'Babies don't feel pain'.
Still, I was the last and first
she saw when the sleep mask
came, when she awoke.

After she split her head on holiday
and needed five stitches,
all the white coats and nurses
ordered me to wait outside.
She remained sitting on my lap.

Later, at a bus stop, when she still signed,
she stared and pointed at a poster
of a baby in an incubator:
a tube taped to one cheek,
the ECG pads on the small chest.

She held my gaze, almost staring,
though by then, I'd got used to cupping
her face in my hands, as she didn't turn
when I called her name. Then, she pointed
her toddler's index finger to herself.

My Daughter's Knight

One winter's night, I found myself sitting
under the great ancestral tree.
Old photos were framed and tied
to the branches with brightly coloured ribbons.
Faces glinted from a light source unseen.

Hanging within reach were familiar motifs:
grandfather's Mexican revolution medal,
grandmother's hand-made lace, a miniature
of my mother's baby grand, another
of my father's tank from the Spanish Civil war.

Among the orchids I picked up
a knight's helmet, dusted it, tried it on.
Though heavy, it fitted. I polished it,
oiled the visor's hinges. Nearby
unsheathed from its scabbard,

a sword gleamed, finest Toledo steel,
light and good for my height. I followed
its movements in a sparring dance,
against an invisible foe. Then, I approached
a horse that neighed and stomped

when he saw me. After a few attempts,
encouraged by family and the instruction
of the newly-minted acronym
of her syndrome, I mounted, took
the reins, her name blazing in my banner.

II) Icons

Black Madonna in Wood Green Shopping City

Our Lady of Guadalupe rises,
held up by a smiling cherub,
a black crescent at her feet.

I grew up with her everywhere;
above my bed, at school,
hanging in car and truck mirrors,

but I've never seen her here in Gift World,
so far from her Basilica, lit up
by fluorescent lights as she floats

above dolphins, circling over fake flowers,
shoppers like pilgrims milling around.
She takes me to the birth country within,

where the orange haze hangs
over the city, volcanoes rising
from the valley to heaven.

¡Ay Dios mío!

(After Alma Lopez's digital collage of Our Lady of Guadalupe)

¡Ay Dios mío! I can't breathe, not after seeing
Our Lady like this, no doubt I'll go to hell.
¡Jesús, María y José, Holy Mother of God!
I can't stop looking, she's almost naked,
she's wearing a bikini of leaves & roses,
(the flowers a nod to the legend of how she
first appeared), and there's a single white bloom
between *(¡Ay!)* her private and sacred virgin's thighs.
Where's the one I grew up with: head bent,
gazing down, covered up, hands praying?
¡Qué sacrilegio! I hear the chorus
of traditional voices shouting,
including mother and *abuelita*,*
que en paz descansen, may they rest in peace.
Our Lady has walked through a portal of light,
she stands looking at me, hands on hips,
long dark hair down her back,
her brown body strong and toned.
¡Mírala nomás! Look at her! I bet she works out.
The cloak draped on her shoulders is now
stamped with Aztec symbols, why does she
remind me of someone ready to fight?
Holding up a crescent moon at her feet, *¡híjole!*
a bare-breasted woman with butterfly wings,
what happened to the original cherub?

Our Lady holds my gaze   how do I address her / *¿Usted? ¿Tú?*
Forgive me   perdóname / I take a deep breath /

Yes I know you are a symbol / of womanhood to all Mexican women / **Yes** you represent virginity / dignity and modesty / **Yes** you are *abnegada* self-sacrificing / **Yes** *tu aguantas* you endure / *En silencio* in silence / **Yes** you are the patron of Latin America / held up in a banner at the front / of independence and revolution protests /

After all these decades on Earth / how I wish that when I was younger / I'd looked up to this new Our Lady / I'd never have put up with the abuse / of those handsome clever and mad men /

She embraces me as she speaks /

'Go, *Mija**, your life is sacred / enjoy living it well / Honour yourself / It is fine to be different / Do not be afraid of anyone or anything / Honour the Earth and build loving communities / Speak your truth calmly'

She smiles her Tonantzin Mother Earth smile.

**abuelita:* granny   * *Mija:* my daughter

Malintzin Tenépal, Malinalli: Revised

Most Mexicans call me la chingada / the damned / screwed / fucked up mother / Most Mexicans vilify me as that treacherous woman / that betrayed her country to the conquistadores / Ha! / How convenient! / They think Mexico would not have been conquered / if I hadn't worked for Cortés / POR FAVOR / P-L-E-A-S-E / The Spaniards had horses and firepower and were sick for gold / What did the Mexica have? / Bows and arrows / and lots of gold / We all believed the prophecies / of the coming of the gods and the end of time / I was eight when my father died / then my mother remarried and sold me to another tribe / so that her son would inherit everything / If they want to blame someone / blame her / she betrayed me / I was an educated noble / then I became a slave / I needed to survive / I had no loyalty to the tribe I came from / nor the one I was sold to nor to the Mexica / But that's landed me in the blame / How convenient to say it's always the woman's fault / that she's an evil and scheming temptress / responsible for everything / What would those who must have a scapegoat / have done in my place? / I sometimes get together with those other bad examples of womanhood / Eve / Tiamat / Ishtar and Lilith and we try to figure out how women are both sources of life and blame / Yes / they say I am a shameful and infamous whore / the founding mother of a nation of bastards by bearing Cortés' son / the first mestizo or mixed-race son of Mexico / But I wasn't the first *india* to have a child by a Spaniard / though that is the enduring narrative / Most people don't know that after I bore his son / Cortés sent him to Spain and when he returned / my own son rejected me / his own mother / Then Cortés married me off / to one of his soldiers / I had served my purpose and he married someone who suited him better / So / I am the twisted mother of the country / So / Mexican women are my tainted daughters / How useful for colonising our minds / It's a wonder any woman rises above this mind-fuck / I do wish people would get over their *malinchismo* / me as the stereotype for betraying the *patria* / the motherland / me as the guilty and treacherous one / the deceiver / No I don't want thanks / but I think it's time to see me in a different light / not as victim / but as someone who responded the best way she could / to extraordinary circumstances / without complying with the traditional roles / of virgin / mother / wife and patriot / After all / how many *cabrones* have betrayed and keep betraying Mexico? / But no one says a bad word about them / You know what makes me more sad than angry / that a nation with such a powerful imagination / has been stuck in this prejudice for so long /

Pero no te chinga! *Fucks me off it does*

In the Names of la Santa Muerte

Her skull wears a wig of long, black hair;
her skeleton a cloak, cobalt-blue
strewn with stars. The altar below
is laden with candles, money, toys.

La Milagrosa, the Miraculous One,
wreathed with fresh marigolds,
plastic roses and paper pompoms,
weighed down with gold and silver,
milagros of hearts and limbs.

La Flaquita, the Skinny One,
tattooed on chests and backs.
Her mural painted in most jails.
Hit men offer contracts,
victims pray for justice.

La Niña Santa, the Holy Girl,
carries a scythe and a globe,
she's *Mictecacihuatl*,
she's *Coatlicue*,
Aztec queens of the after-life.

La Niña Blanca, the White Girl.
The first of the month, her day.
Mariachi bands play. Marijuana burns.
Worshippers bring sugar skulls,
pan de muerto and sweets.

La Señora Negra, the Black Lady,
the sovereign, presiding over the shoot outs,
the beheaded of corpses,
the piled-up skulls,
as she reigns, unchallenged, all over Mexico.

Milagros or miracles: miniatures of parts of the body that a person is praying to be healed: a heart, an arm, a leg...
Mariachis: Mexican orchestras that play Mexican music.
Pan de Muerto: a bread that is associated with the Day of the Dead

Duel Between the Quetzalcoatl and Tezcatlipoca

Poised in the twilight between their realms
between the gold and the gloom,
the sun and the moon, the flame and the blue
their eyes are fixed on each other
ears pulled back, fur bristling on the jaguar,
feathers fanned on the serpent,
waiting, neither moving a muscle
each held by the other's fierceness
then pouncing on their rival,
they're all maws and sharp teeth,
striking with muscle fang and claw
a snarling ball, stopping starting
in a constant fight that favours neither
this is how they duel and dwell in and around us
in a constant fight that favours neither
a snarling ball, stopping starting
striking with muscle fang and claw
they're all maws and sharp teeth,
then pouncing on their rival,
each held by the other's fierceness
waiting neither moving a muscle
feathers fanned on the serpent,
ears pulled back, fur bristling on the jaguar,
their eyes are fixed on each other,
the sun and the moon, the flame and the blue,
between the gold and the gloom,
poised in the twilight between their realms.
(Aztec: Quetzalcoatl: The Plumed Serpent, Lord of Light; Tezcatlipoca: The Jaguar, Lord of Night)

Itztli Tezcatl*

I

The volcano's cooled and solid blood lies
inside the earth, where it becomes black,
light brown or green-gold glass,
sometimes mottled-brown, cloudy or
with a golden or silver sheen.

Tezcachiuhqui, the mirror stone craftsman,
first abraded the lustrous surface
with sand, then carved it and polished it
with a cane, to avoid cuts from flaked edges.
Obsidian was the 'talking stone', used for scrying.

The glossy darkness reflects a face,
familiar yet not. The image becomes
far & near ancestors, my daughter, partner,
relatives, friends, colleagues, neighbours and
strangers, each looking back from their realms.

But I want to gaze at my reflection
before the gods cast a spell
and breathed on the stone's surface
to cloud our vision
and separate us from them.

II

Who's looking in?
Who's looking back?
Whose reflection makes me avert my eyes?
Who's hard to recognise, safer to hold at arm's length?
Whose is the face of fear?

I have been *despojada/* stripped, but
I carried on *desgranando/* sorting
(which sometimes made me *sangrar/* bleed)
and still I sifted through what was done,
still is, after layers of centuries.

I have looked at *lo heredado/*   what we inherit
lo adquirido/   what we acquire
lo impuesto/   what is imposed.
But now I need to look
in the eyes of the one

who bridges
the 'either this or that',
embraces
'this and that and that too'.
I wait to gaze at my original reflection.

---

*Obsidian Mirror: Nahuátl, the most widely spoken indigenous language in Mexico

III) Earth

Riviera Maya

I will not describe how the horizon
is crowded with cranes constructing more
of these thousand-room pyramids.

I will not mention the guests who fly
there for sun and those who serve them,
depend on rain water from the wells.

I will not question those who still tell stories
of how, after a drought, the Mayans fled,
how the jungle has smothered their pyramids.

I will not ask the Giant Sea Turtle,
sacred Akumal, the manatees and
the coral reef, why they fear the waters.

I will not say why the growl of the jaguar
is no longer heard as the jungle is
hacked back and bulldozed to build more hotels.

I will not write about any of these because
this is a poem about water.
I am writing about water.

The Axolotl

Its headdress of gills and filaments
        undulates in the water
as it walks towards me on small legs.

        This one is wild, gold speckles
on brown and olive skin, not captive pink or white.
        The eyes are lidless, fixed on me.

I hear the echo of its call rising
        from its ancient home in the wetlands
of the Xochimilco canals in the DF.

        But through the bushes, orchards and trees:
children running, women hanging laundry,
        the makeshift skyline of advancing millions.

They were named after Xolotl, the Aztec god
        of lightning that leads souls to the underworld.
If the axolotls are gone, who guides us now?

DF: Mexico City

Exiled Monarchs

I keep hearing their million wings
like pages turning in the wind
or dry tinder catching.
From the denuding forest,
their insistent fluttering grows,
flickering orange dust on lashes.
Their bright hunger among the stumps
guides me until I find

two satellite pictures:
a few years ago, rare fir trees
were still the winter grounds
for Monarch butterflies.
Today, the stripped land is a blood stain
around the spine of Mexican mountains.

Tlililtzin/ Campanitas/ Morning Glory

My hands pray through the water towards them,
as sunlight shifts the petals from violet
to mauve to blue flame, the corolla
marked by a purple star. This *trepadora*,
this twining climber that feeds the whirring
Pink Spotted and Hummingbird Hawk moths.

For my ancestors, the seeds spoke
with a strong medicine spirit
that granted sacred visions and journeys,
in the realms of angels and gods.

In Nahuatl, *Tlililtzin*, in Spanish, *Campanitas*.
These little bells, dismissed in childhood
as weeds, crying from their luminous throats
for those who perished, for our lost knowledge.

Wall

I will not describe those who die each year
crossing the Sonoran Desert,
from lack of water, sunstroke, wild beasts, *coyotes*.

I will not describe the desert litter
of discarded shoes, clothes, kids' backpacks,
empty plastic bottles and ladders,

the gun shell casings from the *Migra*,
the snorkels for swimming the Rio Grande.
I will not question those who weave the image

of the Virgin of Guadalupe in strips
of paper through the metal posts of the wall,
so that it is visible from both sides.

I will not question the naked, female torso
painted on a teal and turquoise background,
to remember the women killed in Tijuana.

I will not describe how someone taps, raps, bangs,
hits, knocks and pounds with his hands and sticks
the high steel beams, the colour of dried blood.

I will not question how another has brought down
the sky and painted the beach and sea, so that
seen from afar, part of the wall will vanish.

Coyotes: smugglers of illegal immigrants   *Migra*: US Border Patrol

Dark Earth

Matter   Materia   Mater   Madre   Mother

We who carry the weight of the dark earth,
remind you of your loss of reverence for her,
how we live among the sick fruits of such lack:

Materia   Madre

    her poisoned air and waters,
    her continents strip-mined,
       her forests felled.

Mater   Materia

We who carry the weight of the dark earth,
remind you she is not lifeless matter,
she's not here for your God-given right

Madre

to lay cement tongues that speak of your progress,
to abuse, plunder and rape her and her creatures,
       she gives us life.

Mother   Matter

We who carry the weight of the dark earth,
remind you she is our first mother,
when she is in pain, we all suffer.

Madre Materia

Mater

We who carry the weight of the dark earth,
remind you that you have sacrificed
our living mother for your worship of profit.

Mater

We who have been carrying the weight of the dark earth,
we, sons and daughters of the corn creation myths,
whose sacred duty is to guard the earth, we ask you,

Matter Madre

when are you going to join us and take care of her?
How are you going to honour your mother?
When are you going to honour the earth?

Matter Materia Mater Madre Mother

Arctic Circle

Tanning renders the skin
of the animal flat,
like a map where we might
fall off the edges,
so stiff it might never
enfold a child's body
to protect them.

Day and night, Sami women
soften leather with their hands,
knowing this is the sole skin
that shields from the world,
knowing that when it is done,
it is freely given, it is how
love yields us to another.

Blessing Spring 2020

While you queue for food
medicines or to send
supplies to a loved one
you won't see for weeks
may you stand

under a blue sky
in dazzling sunlight
and breathe in deeply
the air now cleaner
while you remember

all those who cannot
and those attending them.
May a flowering
Cherry tree give itself
to your contemplation

as its early blooms shed
more and more petals
that the breeze blows
before laying them
in soft heaps on the ground.

But with time you may
also notice nearby
that the willow's
greening branches mourn
their swish like a veil.

ACKNOWLEDGEMENTS

Thank you to the editors who chose the following poems or versions of them, which appeared in the following:

Blessing 2020, chosen for Festival of Latin American Women Artists' Dance video in Facebook, June 2020.
Wall; Dark Earth and Malintzin Tenépal, Malinalli: Revised, *Un Nuevo Sol* anthology, flipped eye, 2019.
Watching Mother's Ninety-Year-Old Heart, *Is it hot in here or is it me?* anthology, Beautiful Cadaver, Pittsburgh, US, 2019.
Considerations when Curating the past, joint winner Dilemma competition, *Poetry News*, 2017.
Born in the Year of the Dragon and My Daughter's Knight, from *Dragon Child* pamphlet, Acumen, 2015.
Black Madonna, *There are no Strangers* anthology, New Gallery Books, 2015.
Arctic Circle, *The Reader magazine*, 2012.
Exiled Monarchs, *The Visitors* anthology, Cinnamon Press, 2010.

ABOUT THE AUTHOR:

Marina Sánchez is a Latinx mix of Native American/Spanish/British living in London. She is an award-winning poet and translator, widely published in literary journals. Her poems been placed in many national and international competitions and then anthologised. Her debut pamphlet *Dragon Child* (Acumen, 2014), was Book of the Month in the poetry kit website and was featured in the British Library's The Hidden Surprises of Poetry Pamphlets Event (2019). Some of her poems are included in *Un Nuevo Sol* (Flipped Eye, 2019), the first UK Latinx anthology. For more information please go to her poetry p f pages.

ABOUT VERVE POETRY PRESS

Verve Poetry Press is a quite new and already award-winning press that focused initially on meeting a local need in Birmingham - a need for the vibrant poetry scene here in Brum to find a way to present itself to the poetry world via publication. Co-founded by Stuart Bartholomew and Amerah Saleh, it now publishes poets from all corners of the UK and beyond - poets that speak to the city's varied and energetic qualities and will contribute to its many poetic stories.

Added to this is a colourful pamphlet series, many featuring poets who have performed at our sister festival - and a poetry show series which captures the magic of longer poetry performance pieces by festival alumni such as Polarbear, Matt Abbott and Geraldine Carver.

In 2019 the press was voted Most Innovative Publisher at the Saboteur Awards, and won the Publisher's Award for Poetry Pamphlets at the Michael Marks Awards.

Like the festival, we strive to think about poetry in inclusive ways and embrace the multiplicity of approaches towards this glorious art.

www.vervepoetrypress.com
@VervePoetryPres
mail@vervepoetrypress.com